ALL AROUND THE WORLD

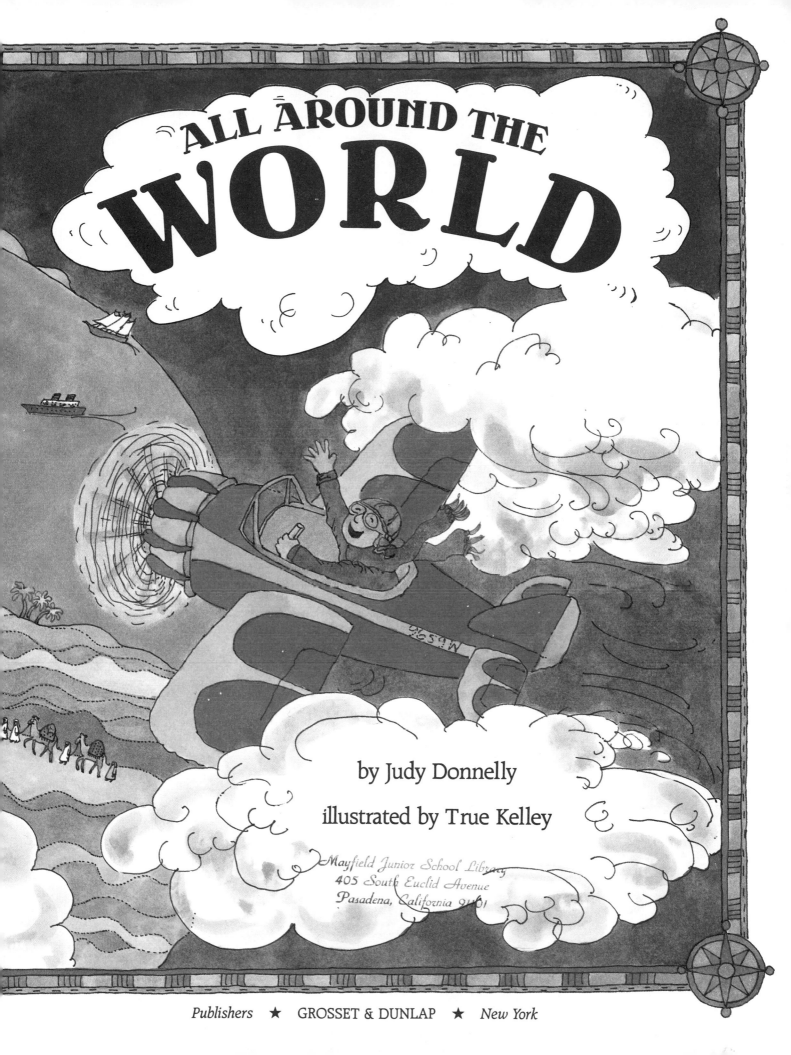

ALL AROUND THE
WORLD

by Judy Donnelly

illustrated by True Kelley

Publishers ★ GROSSET & DUNLAP ★ New York

Today we know the Earth is round, like a ball. But long, long ago almost everyone thought the world was flat, like a plate. Sailors were afraid to sail too far from shore. A ship might reach the edge of the world and fall off!

Once land was out of sight, anything might happen—or so sailors said. They told scary stories about whirlpools that sucked whole ships to the ocean bottom. There were tales of huge sea monsters and mermaids who tricked captains into crashing their ships onto rocks.

So most people stayed close to home. But not everyone. A few brave explorers sailed from island to island, always daring to go a little farther.

Then, in the 1400s, the idea of a round world caught on.

Christopher Columbus believed in a round world. He hoped to find a new, fast way to go from Europe to the rich lands of the Indies. Instead of taking the long, overland route east, he wanted to go by ship in the opposite direction—west. He knew he would have to sail far from land. He would have to cross mysterious seas to reach the Indies. But, as long as the world was round, he was sure he'd get there.

The trouble was that the world was much bigger than Columbus knew. And something was smack in the middle of his route — America! Columbus never got where he meant to go, but his voyage in 1492 gave other explorers the courage to go even farther.

One of these explorers was named Ferdinand Magellan. In 1519 he set off from Portugal to sail all the way around the world. He left with five ships and 280 men. For many months they sailed on. They ran out of food and ate leather, sawdust, and even rats to keep from starving. Magellan died on this voyage. But, after three years, one of his ships and thirty-five men finally made it home again. They were the first humans to circle the Earth. At last, there was proof that the world was round.

MAGELLAN'S VOYAGE

Map-makers learned a lot from Magellan's voyage. But there was still much they didn't know about the world. What was in the far north? What lay to the south? Explorers set out to find the answers. As more and more was learned, map-makers were able to make better and better maps.

There was one problem that was hard to solve. Flat maps couldn't give a really true picture of the round world. So map-makers began making small round models of the Earth—globes.

One of the world's first globes was finished in 1492, the year Columbus landed in America.

First, a map-maker drew a map of the world on long strips of paper with pointed ends. Then the strips were carefully pasted onto a hollow ball, so that they fit together perfectly.

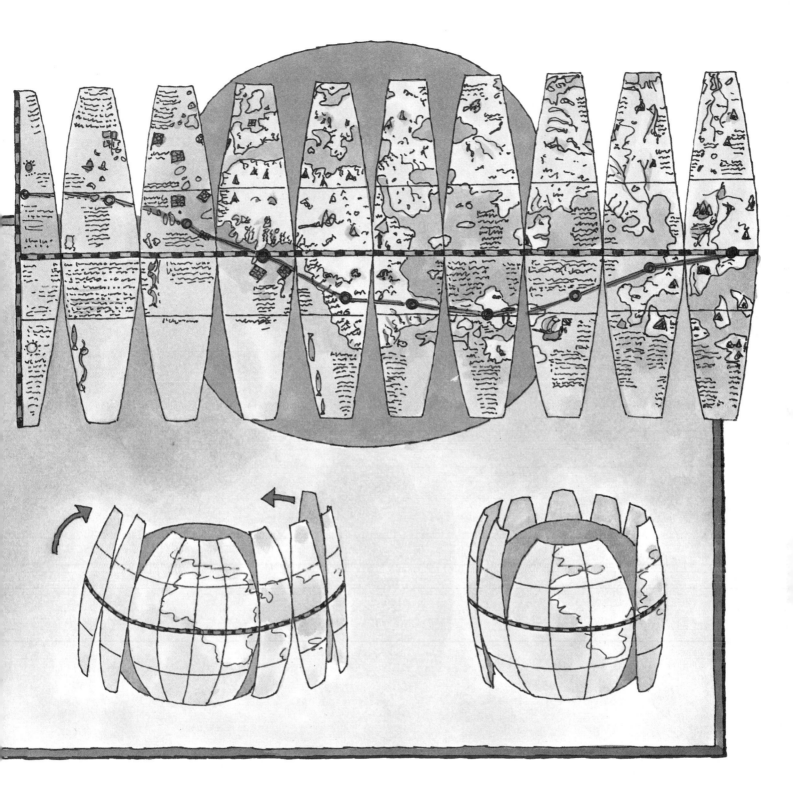

Today some globes are still made this way. But there is a big difference between old-time globes and modern ones. Old globes were full of mistakes. Now globe-makers can copy photographs taken from airplanes and spacecraft. These photographs show every wiggle and squiggle there is in the world.

Just as a model car is small compared to a real car, a globe is very tiny compared to the Earth. In fact, it is about 30 or 40 million times smaller than the Earth. But the globe is still an accurate 3-D model—almost as if the Earth were shrunk down to a handy size. Like model toys or dollhouse furniture, globes are made to *scale.* That means an inch on a globe always stands for a certain number of miles. Scale lets people figure out how far it is from one place to another.

The small size of a globe is one reason people need maps. A map can show a country, a town, a neighborhood, or even one street. Maps can show people exactly how to get from one place to another. Globes don't show these smaller areas clearly, but they do give the truest picture of Earth as a whole.

On a flat map some parts of the world look bigger than they really are, some smaller. Distances are hard to judge, too. Sometimes places that are close together look far apart on a flat map.

The oceans surround huge areas of land called *continents.* Up until the 1700s only five continents had been discovered—Asia, Europe, Africa, South America, and North America.

Map-makers believed there was one more continent in the southern part of the world. They were wrong. There were actually *two* more continents!

Around 1770 European explorers landed on the continent of Australia. About fifty years later explorers found still another continent—Antarctica. But they only reached the edges of it. Antarctica is a continent of ice and snow, the coldest place in the world.

THE PAST

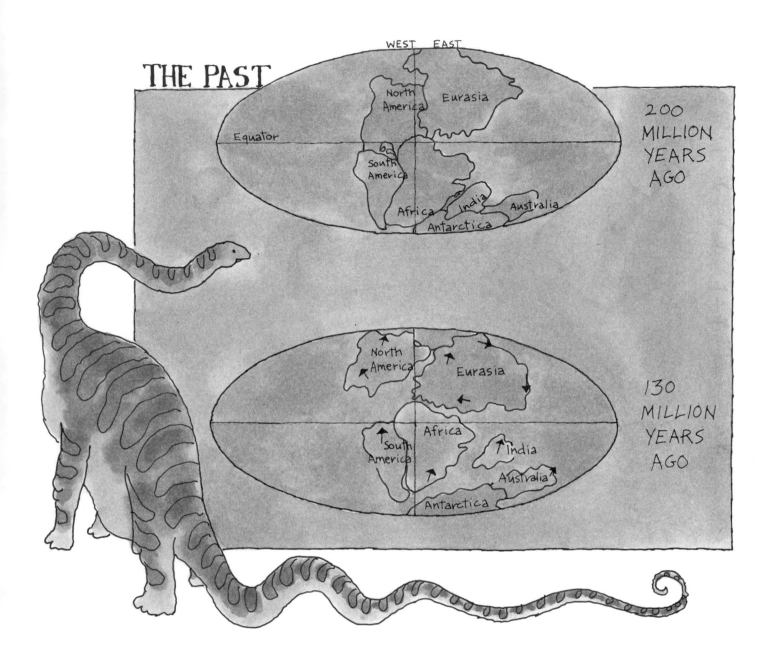

Once, many millions of years ago, the seven continents were all joined together. If you look at Africa and South America, you can see their coastlines fit together almost like pieces in a jigsaw puzzle. Scientists believe that the continents began to separate about 200 million years ago—in the time of the dinosaurs. Very slowly, they drifted apart until they reached their present-day positions. The continents are still moving apart—about three-quarters of an inch every year—so that millions of years from now the continents will be in very different places.

TODAY

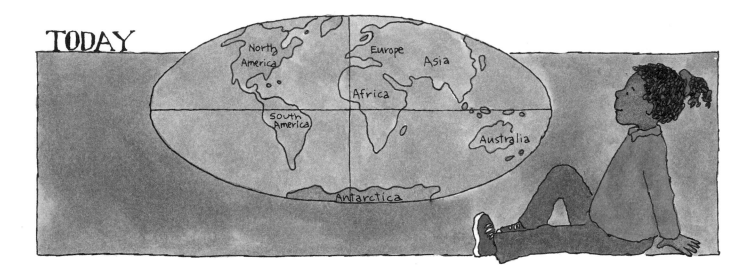

THE FUTURE

50 MILLION YEARS FROM NOW

100 MILLION YEARS FROM NOW

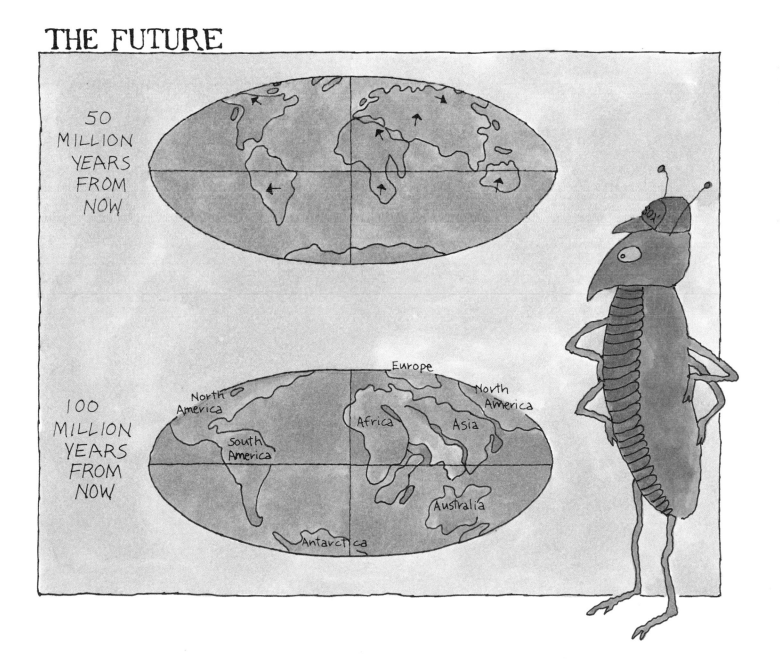

Take a look at a globe. You will see a line that goes all around the middle of the Earth. This line is called the equator. Of course, there isn't really a line like this on the Earth. But map-makers use the equator to divide the world in half. That's where the word equator comes from: the halves are equal.

Brrrr!

North Pole

How fat is the world? If you tied a ribbon around the equator, it would be more than 24,000 miles long.

SOUTH

It is very hot along the equator. But it gets colder and colder the farther you travel from it. Both the very top of the world — the North Pole — and the very bottom — the South Pole — are freezing! Temperatures are different in different parts of the world because of the way the rays of the sun hit the Earth.

The Earth travels in a big circle around the sun. It takes the Earth 365 days—or one year—to make this trip. Scientists believe the Earth is 4½ billion years old. So that means the Earth has gone around the sun 4½ billion times!

NEPTUNE

MARS

VENUS

URANUS

JUPITER

The Earth is one of nine planets that circle the sun. Mercury is closest to the sun. Pluto is the farthest away.

While the Earth travels around the sun, it is moving in another way, too. It spins like a top, around and around. It takes 24 hours—one day—for the Earth to make one complete spin.

Only the half of the Earth that faces the sun is lit up by the sun's rays. We call that day. The half that is facing away from the sun is dark. We call that night.

While you are going to sleep, children on the other side of the world are just waking up! Shine a flashlight on a globe. Turn the globe slowly, and you can see how the sun makes day and night.

If you fly over the Earth in an airplane, the land looks mostly green and brown. So why does your globe look like a patchwork of rainbow colors? These patches of pink and green and yellow and orange show how the continents are divided into different countries.

Dotted lines on a globe show exactly where one country ends and another begins. These are *borders* or *boundaries*. There are no dotted lines on Earth, but sometimes countries build walls along their borders. Sometimes a desert or a river or a mountain separates one country from another.

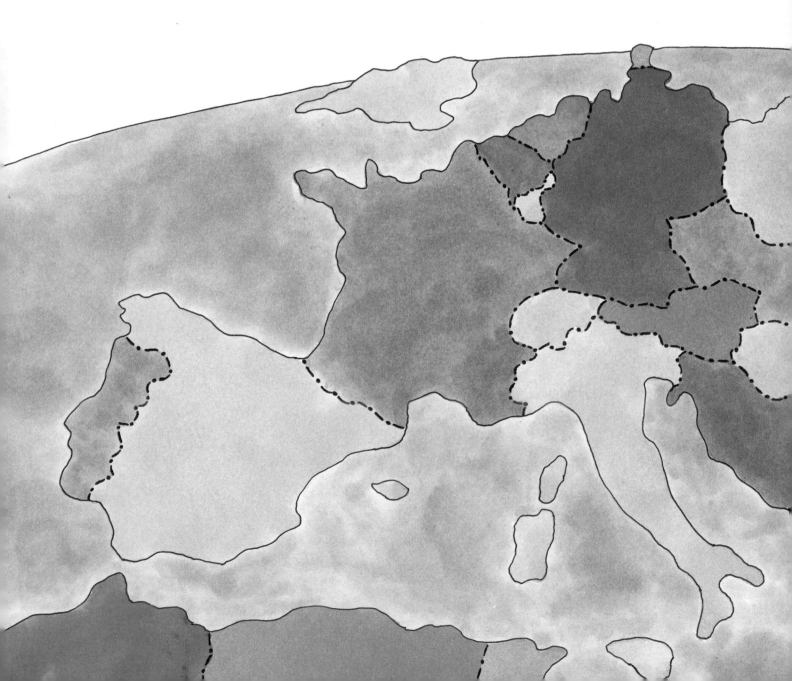

Globes made even fifty years ago show a world that is different from the world today. Countries have changed their names. Countries have changed their borders. The United States is more than three times as big as it was 200 years ago!

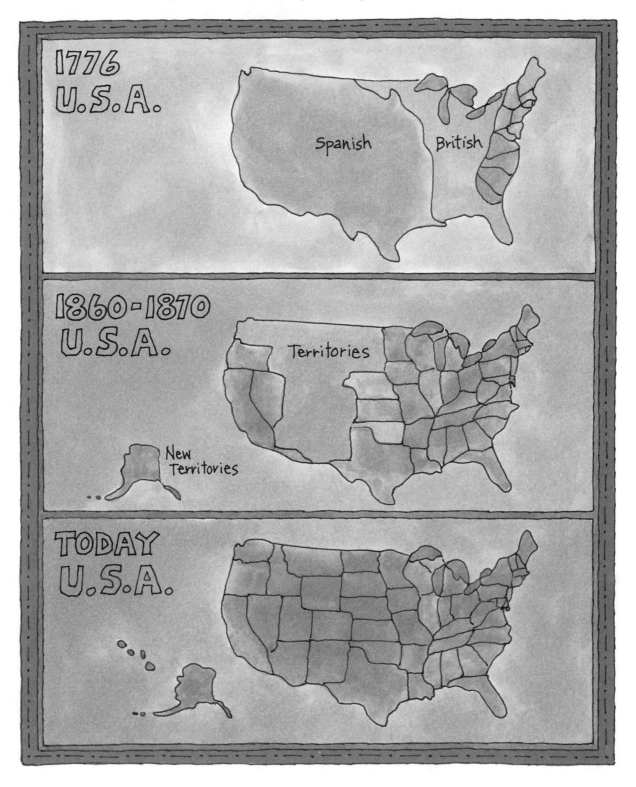

There are over 150 countries today. But perhaps one day people will decide not to divide the world into countries at all. Everyone will just belong to planet Earth.

Some Map and Globe Words

border or boundary: the dividing line between countries or other areas of land

continent: one of seven large areas of land on Earth

country: an area of land with its own government

day: the time it takes for the Earth to make one complete turn

equator: an imaginary line around the middle of the Earth

North Pole: the most northern point on Earth

oceans: huge bodies of salt water that cover three-quarters of the Earth

scale: the size of a model or a map compared to the real thing

South Pole: the most southern point on Earth

year: the time it takes the Earth to circle the sun